Anonymous

A review of Dr. Newman's Apologia pro vita sua

Anonymous

A review of Dr. Newman's Apologia pro vita sua

ISBN/EAN: 9783337773533

Printed in Europe, USA, Canada, Australia, Japan

Cover: Foto ©ninafisch / pixelio.de

More available books at **www.hansebooks.com**

A

REVIEW

OF

DR. NEWMAN'S,

APOLOGIA PRO VITA SUA.

LONDON:

W. DUFF, PRINTER, 256, PENTONVILLE ROAD. N.

From an early age, up to the period when he became a Roman Catholic Priest, Dr. Newman appears to have been the passive victim of many fortuitous influences, and as many transitory impressions; all of them from sources, purely human.

At fourteen years of age, he read Paine's Tracts against the Old Testament; some of Hume's Essays, and copied some French verses against the immortality of the soul. He appears to have been struck with the plausibility of some of those writings, but was not biassed by them.

At fifteen - - -" a great change of thought took place in him. He fell under the influence of a definite Creed, and received into his intellect, impressions of dogma." Those intellectual impressions were not received from a study and meditation of the Word of God, but from some works, "all from the School of Calvin." From one of Mr. Romaine's works, Dr. Newman " received at once, the doctrine of final perseverance."

Dr. Newman soon abandoned " the detestable doctrine" of election and final perseverance; not from any light he had received from the Scriptures, but from the works of " the writer who made a deeper impression on his mind than any other— Thomas Scott, of Aston Sandford who planted deep in his mind, that fundamental Truth of religion" - - - - belief in the Holy Trinity.

In the autumn of 1816, Dr. Newman received *another* "deep impression." Not from reading the Word of God, "but from two other works, each contrary to each, and planting in him, the seeds of an intellectual inconsistency, which disabled him for a long course of years."

These were, Milner's Church history, and Newton on the prophecies.

p. 62 In the same season and year, "another deep imagination (*sic*) took possession of him,—there could be no mistake about the fact;—viz, that it was the will of God that Dr. Newman should lead a single life."

In the year 1822, Dr. Newman "came under very different influences from those to which he had hitherto been subject." From a Dr. Hawkins, "he learnt to weigh his words and to be cautious in his statements, and to clear his sense in discussion and controversy." "Then as to doctrine," Dr. Hawkins, but not the word of God, "was the means of great additions to his belief." He gave him Sumner's Treatise on apostolical Preaching; from reading which, Dr. Newman learnt to "give up his remaining Calvinism," and to receive the doctrine of Baptismal Regeneration; while from a Mr. Blanco White, Dr. Newman "was led to p. 65. have freer views on the subject of inspiration, than were usual in the Church of England, at that time."

But "there is another *principle*, which I gained from Dr. Hawkins, "says Dr. Newman," *more directly* bearing upon Catholicism, than *any other* that I have Italics our own mentioned, and that is the doctrine (*sic*) of Tradition." Dr. Hawkins' sermon on the subject, "made a most serious impression upon me," observes Dr. Newman, so serious indeed, that he at once assented to the "self-evident proposition" "that the sacred text was never intended to teach doctrine, but only to prove it, and that if we would learn doctrine, we must have recourse to the formularies of the Church; for instance, to the Catechism. and to the Creeds." "This view continues Dr. Newman, most true in its outline, most fruitful in its consequence, opened upon me a large field of thought." At a subsequent period, influenced by this view, Dr.

Newman withdrew his name from the Bible Society. p. 66
The word of God being thus disposed of, as not intended to teach any one doctrine, but simply to prove
Creeds and formularies, we are, nevertheless led to
infer and to expect, that Dr. Newman would indeavour
to verify and prove all the doctines he has learnt, and
believes in, by the Sacred Text.

In 1823, Dr. Newman was "taught the doctrine of
apostolical Succession by a Fellow of Oriel; in the
course of a walk," he believes, "round Christ Church
meadow." p. 67.

Dr. Newman supposes that "it was about this time
also, "that he read Butler's Analogy; the study of
which "was an era (*sic*) in his religious views." p. 67.

On the next page, Dr. Newman records the fact, that
from Dr. Whately, he learnt that the Church was a sub-
stantive body or corporation." Dr. Whately also "fixed
in him those anti Erastian views of Church polity which
were one of the most prominent features of the Tractarian movement." p. 69.

In the year 1826, he became acquainted with Mr.
Keble, known by name to many of the upper classes
in this country, and who, Dr. Newman states, "was
the true and primary author" of the Tractarian movement. From Mr. Keble, whom he then called "his
new master", and not from the Word of God, Dr. Newman learned "two main intellectual truths." One was
the "Sacramental System;" and the other, as far as
can be made out, a modified way of appreciating
Butler's doctrine, that Probability is the guide of life.

Dr. Newman's next teacher was a Mr. Hurrell
Froude. "he was a man" says Dr. Newman, of the
highest gifts." "A man of high genius, brimfull and over-
flowing with ideas and views, in him original, which
were too many and strong, even for his bodily strength,

and crowded and jostled each other in their efforts after distinct shape and expression, with an intellect as critical and logical, as it was speculative and bold." As thus described, Mr. Froude's intellectual or mental condition, was one we should have deemed it charitable to make some attempt to order and to adjust. To say or believe, that he was a man of genius is a mistake. He was one whose ideas had not been derived from the word of God, but were, as Dr. Newman says, " in him original" and which could not, nevertheless, attain to distinct shape and expression, notwithstanding his critical and logical turn of mind; enfeebled moreover, by a strong speculative tendency. The Scriptures say, that "the *wisdom* of this World is foolish with God;" and " the Scriptures cannot be broken." From Mr. Froude however and not from the Scriptures, Dr. Newman learned "to look with admiration towards the Church of Rome, and in the same degree to dislike the Reformation." *He* fixed deep in me," says Dr. Newman, " the *idea* of devotion to the blessed Virgin, and *he* led me gradually to believe in the Real Presence." Here it may be fairly observed, that Dr. Newman ought, according to the doctrine he learned from Dr. Hawkins, to have searched the Scriptures, and endeavoured to prove, as did the Bereans— "*who searched the Scriptures daily*," whether Mr. Froude followed, or attempted to follow the example of the apostle Paul, who "reasoned "with the Jews of Thessalonica, "*out of the Scriptures*." But St. Paul was "a servant of *Jesus Christ*;" called to be an apostle, not of *men*, neither *by* man but by the will of God, and separated unto the gospel of God. Further on, Dr. Newman states that he cannot specify the particular period " when he first learnt to consider that *antiquity* was the true exponent of the doctrine of Christianity, and the basis of the Church of England." He takes it for granted however

p. 35.

Acts XVII. 2

Rom. 1.1.
Gal. 1.1.

that he learnt this from reading the works of Bishop
Bull. p. 88.

After his return to Oxford, from a tour on the Continent, Dr. Newman commenced a series of papers,
known by the Title of Tracts for the Times. From
1834 to 1836, he was more or less engaged in writing
a book on " The Prophetical Office of the Church,
viewed relatively to Romanism and Popular Protest-
antism." In this volume Dr. Newman did not write
in favor of Romanism; rather the contrary. It was an
attempt at commencing a system of theology " (*sic*) not
*upon the foundation of the apostles and prophets,
Jesus Christ himself being the corner-stone,* but "on Eph.c. 11.20
the Anglican idea, and based upon Anglican authorities"! Dr. Newman wished to build up an Anglican p. 141
theology out of the stones which already lay cut and
hewn upon the ground, the past toil of great divines." p. 142

In 1837, he wrote an Essay on Justification; not
with the object of shewing and developing that which
the Prophets had said, and foresaid about it, nor what
the Lord himself and his apostles have said and taught
on this subject, but Dr. Newman wrote against the
Lutheran doctrine, that Justification by faith only
was the cardinal doctrine of Christianity." p. 151.

In 1838, he wrote a pamphlet with the object of
"placing the doctrine of the Real Presence on an intellectual basis." p. 152.

Dr. Newman translated also Fleury's Church history.
alluding to a particular date or period of his career,
connected with this translation he observes, I mention
it as one of *many* particulars *curiously* illustrating
how truly my change of opinion came, not from foreign
influences, but from the workings of *my own mind,
and the accidents around me.*" p. 154.

Fleury, in his " Customs of the Primitive Christians,

8

makes an important statement, which Dr. Newman does not give any evidence of having paid any practical attention to.

"A portion of the holy books was read," observes Fleury, "after which the Bishop explained the Gospel and the other holy books. The faithful moreover privately studied the law of God; they again read in their own houses, that which they had heard read at Church. Every father, in the midst of his family, acted like a pastor, who presided at the prayers and family readings; instructing his wife, his children and his servants. Several Christians, even among the laity, knew the scriptures by heart, so assiduously did they read them. The women also, did not read them less than the men did."

If Dr. Newman had followed the example of the early Christians, as stated above by Fleury (Roman Catholic Priest), and sought to learn the will of God, by reading his Word, he, Dr. Newman would have discerned how earthly and how worthless, was his "change of opinion", arising from *the workings of his own mind, and the accidents around him.* The only truth that the Lord will acknowledge, consists in believing and following after that which *He* hath revealed and imposed on his fallen creatures, and not that which *they* are pleased to imagine must, and shall be pleasing to Him.

In 1841, Dr. Newman wrote on the Articles of the Church of England. As heretofore, his object, was not to defend the Anglican Establishment, nor to impugn the doctrines of Romanism. His purpose was "to ascertain the ultimate points of controversy between the Roman and Anglican Creeds, and to make them as few as possible." The Word of God was not in question at all. Neither was it Dr. Newman's object to test either of

Margin: Art. 6. See also Crustit. apost. liv. 2. C. 57. & the 9 apostolical canon.

Margin: p. 180.

the above " systems of theology" by the Scriptures.
He wished to shew that the Articles " but partially op-
pose the Roman dogma;" but partially disclaim, "the
dominant errors," as he then called them, of Rome.
" there was no doubt at all," says Dr. Newman, of the
elasticity of the Articles, I wanted to ascertain what
was the limit of that elasticity, in direction of the
Roman dogma. This Essay or Tract, was met, Dr.
Newman tells us, with a storm of indignation. But conscious, as usual, that his opinions were " the birth of
his own mind, and the *circumstances in which he was
placed*," "I had, he adds " a scorn of the imputations
which were heaped upon me." p. 181.

In 1843, owing to the persevering attacks of the
Bishops, he gave up the Living of St. Mary at Oxford,
and retired to Littlemore, where he had built a Church,
and where at one time he contemplated a monastic
house. At Littlemore, free of anxiety and harass, he
determined to put aside controversy, and commenced
a translation of St. Athanasius. But between July and
November," observes Dr. Newman, "I received three
blows which broke me." p. 243.

The first blow consisted in discovering, " that in the
history of Arianism, the pure Arians were the Protestants, the semi-Arians were the Anglicans, and that
Rome now was what it was. " It is difficult to suppose
what we are expected to infer from this discovery. Neither Arianism, nor semi-Arianism is taught or upheld
in the Anglican Establishment, and it is not easy to
guess why the past evil of a past generation, should be
a motive for going over to Romanism. The second
blow consisted in the attacks of the " Bishops one after
another," chiefly, it appears, on Tract 90. They went
on directing charges against Dr. Newman, for three
years which added much to his " misery," caused by

the first blow. He presented however a determined front, and refused to retract or gainsay anything he had asserted in the Tract.

p. 244.

The third blow was struck by "the affair of the Jerusalem Bishoprics." It caused a great commotion in Dr. Newman's spirit, and was *the* "final blow, which finally shattered his faith in the Anglican Church." While the Anglican Bishops censured him for avowing an approach to the Catholic Church, and not closer than he thought the Anglican formularies allowed, they, the Bishops, · " were fraternizing by their act, or by their sufferance with Protestant bodies, and allowing them to put themselves under an Anglican Bishop, without any renunciation of their errors or regard to the due reception of baptism and confirmation. Dr. Newman sent a formal Protest against the appointment of the first Bishop of Jerusalem, both to his own Diocesan and to the Primate.

p. 245.

In November 1845, he wrote to Cardinal Wiseman to announce his conversion, and " could find nothing better to say to him, that he would obey the Pope as he had obeyed his own Bishops in the Anglican Church."

We are not of those who believe that Dr. Newman is guilty of having at any time, remained in the Anglican Establishment under false pretences. Neither do we believe that he was ever *conscious* of being deceived, or of deceiving others. We believe moreover, that he is sincere and devout in his faith in all that the Papal system imposes. Indeed his assertions on this particular point, are bolder than any Roman Catholic in Rome itself, would like to publish. "I think it impossible" says he, " *to withstand the evidence* which is brought, for the liquefaction of the blood of St. Januarius at Naples, and for the motion of the eyes of the Madonna in the Roman States. I see no reason to doubt

Dr. Newman's Italics

the nature of the Lombard Crown at Mònza; and I *dont see why* the Holy Coat at Tréves may not have been what 'it professes to be. *I firmly believe* that his own Italics parts of the True Cross are at Rome, and elsewhere, that the Crib of Bethlehem is at Rome, and the bodies of St. Peter and St. Paul also." With few exceptions, all Protestants and Papists in this country, and on the Continent of Europe, who deem it worth while to bestow any thought at all on similar things, believe it *quite possible* to question and to disprove the "evidence" of the liquifaction of the blood of St. Januarius. Many see *no reason at all* for beleiving that the Holy Coat at Tréves is that which " *it* " (!) professes to be; and so on. Still we repeat: we have no doubt of Newman's belief in, and devotion for such things; and we believe it to be, practically, nearly equal to that of the Hindoo, who rushes under the wheels of the Car of Jugganat; deeming himself happy, if peradventure, he is not hindered from being crushed to death. He, like Dr. Newman, *sees* no reason to doubt why, he should not, by such faith attain unto a better resurrection. There is *no* limit, to the wickedness, deception, or folly, of devout persons who choose to worship and serve God and his Christ, their own way, without the light and *guidance of His own Word.*

But now as respects Dr. Newman himself, what a poor and humiliating specimen of humanity does the above sketch of his career present! From one man he learns to believe in the Trinity. Another man plants in him, "the seeds of an intellectual inconsistency." From Sumner, he receives the doctrine that infants are regenerated when they are baptized. From a Dr. Hawkins, he learns to believe in the " Doctrine of Tradition", and that "the sacred text was never intended to teach doctrine but to prove it. From a fellow of Oriel he learns the doctrine of "Apostolical Succes-

sion." From 'a Mr. Froude, he is gradually taught to
believe in the "Real Presence," and the *idea* of devotion to the blessed virgin Mary," and so on; leaving
the readers of his Apology to infer that he has learned
nothing from the pages of Scripture. Half a verse however, from a sentence pronounced by the Lord himself,
will shew why Dr. Newman has wasted his life in
trying to reform, adjust, or assimilate Creeds, Formularies, and systems, without reference to the will of
God, as revealed by Himself in his own Word.
 "*Ye do err*" said the Lord Jesus Christ, "*not
knowing the Scriptures.*

It is not easy, or perhaps even possible, to detect from
Dr. Newman's Apology, what it is that he rests his
hopes of acceptance and salvation on. He, e. g. believes
in the need, absolutely, of regeneration, and of a new
birth; but it cannot be made out how he has attained
personal possession and enjoyment of this transform-
ing truth. It is certainly plain that he believes that he
was regenerated when he was baptized. He could not
learn this from the Word of God, not in any one part
of it, because it makes no allusion to such a thing. He
learned this from the Creeds or the Catechism. Good:
but altho he declares that Scripture was especially
intended to *prove* doctrine, he does not prove, or *attempt* to prove from the Scriptures, that he was thus
regenerated in virtue, and by the power of a truth or
promise revealed to him by his Lord and God. He may
explain away this difficulty, by assuring us, that
"Antiquity is the true exponent of the doctrines of
Christianity," and that he believes in the "Doctrine
of Tradition." But altho this does not dispense him
from keeping to his own assertion, that the sacred text
should be brought forward to prove doctrine, he should,
at least, endeavour to *prove* from the word of God, that
which antiquity and Tradition has imposed on his con-

science respecting regeneration by baptism. The real truth however, is, that both Antiquity and Tradition are divided against themselves, respecting every one of the doctrines believed in by the Romanists. Dr. Newman for example, believes in what is called the "Real Presence." As this is purely a human and earthly idea, human Tradition must be sought for to support it. Yet St. Augustine whom Dr. Newman calls, "the great luminary of the West," believed the contrary:

" The holy body of Jesus Christ is as far from the Sacrament as the highest heaven is far above the Earth." *De Civit Dei.*

Dr. Newman also believes in a sort of intermediate place, to which men have given the name of Purgatory.* But here again, what becomes of his opinion or belief, that Tradition must be consulted and trusted to, for some ancient traditions are against him.

"I refuse to believe," declared St. Cyril, that the souls of the faithful go into a place of torment." *In Evang. Job. c. 36.*

St. Bernard also said :

" There are but three places ; Heaven, the Earth, and Hell." *Cours de Theol. de Scharp. p 2005.*

But the Romanists or rather the Roman Priests, believe that the two Fathers, just quoted are wrong ; or if they were once right, the "definition" of the Council of Florence has set their statements and belief aside.

---

* The existence of this place was finally discovered by the Council of Florence, 1438. When convenient Rome not only sets aside the word of God, but brings forward pagan writers, to establish that which is opposed to the letter and spirit of Scripture. Cardinal Bellarmino finding it difficult to uphold the dogma even by perverting Scripture recurs to Plato, Cicero, and Virgil, whom he quotes in support of this "definition." But Purgatory could not be an immense source of revenue without another "definition" establishing the efficacy of prayers and sacrifices for the "holy souls" in course of purgation. We believe that this also was borrowed from the pagans. We had occasion, a few weeks ago, to read through Petronius' Satyricon, a task no one can accomplish without either defiling his spirit, or being vexed with righteous indignation. The following incident however struck us. Habinnas, a petty magistrate of Rome, happening to come in late, at a great feast given by Trimalhion : the former, in answer to an observation on his tardy appearance, replied that he had been engaged in the celebration of a *sacred novena* with Scissa, in behalf of Missellas, one of his slaves, lately deceased. A Novena, or a nine days observance of certain religious exercises, is the commonest way, the Romanists have of obtaining some favor, generally from a *patron Saint.* Those who "are of God" rely on the promises made to them through the Redeemer. "Whatsoever ye ask the *Father* in *my* name he will do it." The reader may learn the extent to which Rome has packed pagan customs and ideas together with some of God's truths, in Middleton's *Letter from Rome.* See also Jean le Croi's *Les Conformites des Cérémonies modernes avec les anciennes* and Josiah Stopford's *Pagano—Papismus.* Some have, with great probability, assumed that Middleton gathered all his information from those works.

Then what becomes of the assertion that Antiquity and Tradition must be taken as a guide and exponent of the will of God? The stereotyped reply is, that when "the Church" declares that a certain traditional doctrine or idea, is to be received as truth, this decision is an infallible one. But here again some Traditions are against this human device:

"Cease to allege unto us," says St. Athanasius, Athan. de Incar. Christ. Epis. Fest. 39. that which is not written: the books of God, suffice for the attainment of all truth; they alone are the school of all godliness; and we desire neither to hear, nor to quote anything but what they contain."

St. Basil Bish: of Cesarea. In. Ascet. def. 72 A.D. 379. "Let us compare the discourses and the writings of our teachers with the doctrines of the Bible, and let us accept that only which is in conformity with the Scriptures."

These and similar quotations, as twenty years experience has taught us, are always got rid of in the usual way: "that the Church is infallible, and does, infallibly, correct, add, subtract, modify, discover improve, and impose new truths and new doctrines, which shall be according to the will of God, without reference to His Scriptures, or to Tradition." But then what becomes of Dr. Newman's distinct assertion that Infallibility *must ever be guided by Scripture* p. 393. *and Tradition?*"

Isaiah. "Their fear of me" said the Lord, "is taught by the precepts of men"—"In *vain* they do worship me, teaching for doctrines the commandment of men." "Thus have ye made the commandments of God of *none* effect, by your tradition;" declared Christ unto the learned Scribes and Pharisees of Jerusalem, when they found fault with His disciples for transgressing the "*tradition of the elders.*" Ignoring these Scriptures however, and avowing implicit belief in the"Doc-

trine of Tradition" Dr. Newman says : "Authority in
its most imposing exhibition, grave bishops, laden
with the traditions and rivalries of particular nations or
places, have been guided in their decisions "—by the
Spirit of God revealing His mind unto them thro the
written Word ? No! "by the commanding genius of in- p. 40.
dividuals; sometimes," adds Newman, "young, and
of inferior rank!" So much for the poor, wretched,
and sinful vanity of man, whenever he attempts to impose his folly on his Creator. The above assertion by
Dr. Newman however, *very accurately* sets forth the
system followed by the Roman Priesthood. It may
be more easily appreciated, by comparing it to the
chest of a sea-faring man. It has been packed, unpacked,
repacked, and provided with requisites for any country
fashion, clime and date, so that the contents may
everywhere suit everything and every body. One recent example is connected with the Virgin Mary. In
ancient times Rome condemned the Collyridians for
praying to the Virgin, and declared them heretics for
so doing, for at that time Rome had not gone so far as
to set aside the commandment which says " Thou shalt
not make unto thyself *any* graven image, or the likeness of *anything* that is in *heaven above,* or that is in
the *earth beneath.* Thou shalt not *bow down thyself*
to them nor *serve* them." Lately however, Rome has
exalted Mary to the highest offices and dignity of a
goddess, before whose image the Romanist bows himself, and worships. But the papists, or rather the
Popish priests say that *both* decrees, for and against,
this practice, were infallible. To which I reply ; "God
is not mocked," as you will find out, in the day of
Judgment, unto your own confusion. No marvel, that
although Dr. Newman states that the sacred text is
intended to prove doctrine, he never once attempts to

do so. Satan at least, did endeavour to prove, by distinct although guileful quotations from the word of God, the lawfulness of his means and motives, for tempting our Lord, and to induce him to prove His Sonship. But although we believe that Dr. Newman has never been *conscious* of deceiving others, he himself has been the darling of some deceiving spirit. If some readers are disposed to deem this statement too strong or uncharitable, I think the following observations will remove both these impressions.

Respecting the lately invented fable that Mary was born without sin, Dr Newman says---" I have no difficulty in receiving it: if I have no difficulty, why not a hundred? a thousand? now I am sure that Catholics in general have not any intellectual difficulty at all on on the subject, and that there is no reason why they should. Priests have no difficulties." The question is not whether poor wretched man has " any difficulty in believing it " or whether a hundred or a thousand, choose to believe it. The important fact is, that the God of heaven says the contrary. As to the intellect: the intellect has nothing to do with it. If the inspired word of God had told us that Mary was conceived free of sin, what presumption for man to talk of his intellect! Dr. Newman however, says there is " not any intellectual difficulty at all on the subject." But if the word of God is totally silent on the subject, and *directly* implies the contrary, there is *every reason* for having *every kind* of intellectual difficulty about it. And here again, why does Dr. Newman neglect to prove this " definition " concerning Mary, by Scripture and Tradition. Against the Lord God, and his plain unchangeable Word, Dr. Newman gets over every difficulty, in these words."There is no difficulty at all in holding that the blessed Virgin Mary was conceived without original sin : indeed it is a simple fact to say, that Catholics

have not come to believe it because it is defined, but p. 394.
it was defined because they believed it." Dr. Newman
may well say, and we may all readily believe, that
" Priests have no difficulties." They never had, or
cared to have any difficulties. But the truth is, that
very few Papists had ever heard of this fable before it p. 17.
was "defined ' and *could not*, therefore, believe it, before it was invented; while three fourths of them do
not believe it at all, now that they *have* heard of it. Dr.
Newman however asserts the contrary, "so far" says he,
" from the definition in 1854 being a tyranical infliction
on the Catholic World, it was received everywhere
on its promulgation with the greatest enthusiasm."
Where and wl en did he hear or learn all this? It is one
of his silly, albeit, sincere assumptions. It is not true.
It is most false. We happened to be near Rome when
this "definition" was proclaimed, and in the same year
traversed the whole of Europe, all Italy and the whole
of the Levant, and altho' we frequently tried, we could
not get a single Roman Catholic to pay any attention
at all to the subject. We do not say that there are no,
"Catholics" who do not bear this "definition" in mind
but we deliberately say, that although we, in a quiet,
perhaps jesuitical way sought to know how it had been
received, we only met with one man out of England who
had bestowed a moment's thought on the subject, and
that man was a Roman Catholic priest, returning from
Nubia with a bevy of negroes en route for Rome. He
distributed a medal of the "immaculate conception" to
all the sailors and to some of the passengers on board.
The former cursed, swore, and derided the whole thing
in the most offensive way. Dr. Newman may verify this
at any time he likes, if he will only doff his priestly
garments, travel about *all over* the Continent, mix with
the people, and test their faith on this "dogma." But

how recklessly Dr. Newman indulges in words and assertions! "The definition in 1854" he tells the English Public, was received *everywhere* with the *greatest enthusiasm.*" Will Dr. Newman, we again ask, take the trouble to inform us where and when he learnt this. Now we ask everybody, excepting a Roman Catholic priest, whether the following observations made by Dr. Newman himself on this subject, do not, *a priori,* convince us that the enthusiasm he speaks of, is a myth.

"Of course," he says, there were grave and good men who were made anxious by the doubt whether it could be proved apostolical, either by Scripture or Tradition, and who accordingly, though believing it themselves, did not see how it could be defined by authority; but this, "adds Dr. Newman, conveniently, "is another matter." "The point in question is, whether the doctrine is a burthen. I believe it to be none." Having answered for himself, Dr. Newman thinks he can also answer for St. Bernard and St. Thomas, and sincerely thinks that "if they were now living, they would have rejoiced to accept it for its own sake." It is in this way, and in such language, that Dr. Newman deals with an invention, which he wishes us to believe, was everywhere received with enthusiasm. Is it too much to assert that he has been, and is, the darling victim of a deceiving spirit? Nearly two thousand years after her birth, a set of Priests, inhabiting Rome, pass a decree, that shall oblige us to believe, must influence the first germs of Mary's existence. The dogma of the immaculate conception of Mary" (whose father was a sinner) was too paltry and sectarian for public or official notice, but it was received with greater contempt than has been bestowed on the Encyclical just issued by the Pope, despised by the masses, and officially ignored by every European Government. Let us now hear how Dr.

p. 394.

p. 395.

Newman talks about new doctrines, and infallibility.

"The new truth which is promulgated, if it be called new, must be at least homogeneous, cognate, implicit, viewed relatively to the old truth." "It must be what *I* may have guessed *(sic)* or wished *(sic)* to be included in the apostolical revelation; and it will be of such a character, that my thoughts readily concur in it, or coalesce with it, as soon as I have heard it, *perhaps (sic)* I and others have always believed it. and the only question which is now decided in my belief, is that I am henceforth to believe that I have only been holding what the apostles held before me"! It is after this fashion that Dr. Newman and the Roman priests impose a new religion on the God of heaven, which they require Him to accept from his fallen creatures. Statements of this sort, are the basis of the *whole* of Dr. Newman's apology.

p. 393.

But it is difficult to conceive how such men can, in the secret of their soul, realize that they must, one day, stand before the judgement seat of Christ. "The word that I have spoken," said the Lord, "the *same* shall judge him in the last day; for I have *not* spoken of *myself*, but the Father which sent me, he gave me commandment, what I should say, and what I should speak, and I know that his commandment is life everlasting: whatsoever I speak therefore, even as the Father saith unto me, so I speak."

John XII.
48—50

But if the word of God, and the remembrance thereof were taken away from the whole Earth, the Roman Priests would not miss it. This is now their glory, and the source of their craft, but in the day of judgement it shall turn unto their own perdition.

Apolog's p.p.
28 and 390

One or two more extracts from Dr. Newman's Appology will show how easily he may be led and misled. His weakness in this respect, appears to us, to consist of a mixture of hysteria, ignorance of self, and of human nature, with a large amount of credulity, which forswears common sense, and the plainest truths of Scripture.

At page 320 he states that while in the Anglican Establishment, he received from the President of Maynooth a bundle of penny or half-penny books of devotion, as they are found in the booksellers shops at Rome. "On looking them over," says Dr. Newman, "I was quite astonished to find how different they were from what *I* had fancied, how little there was in them to which *I* could really object" Now in the first place, Dr. Russell, the President of Maynooth is too astute, and too expert, to fail in selecting the sort of penny books just suited to meet the particular stage which Dr. Newman or any one else, has reached towards "Conversion." Secondly : it is of no moment at all, what Dr. Newman "fancied" they might have been, before he read them; but when he did read them, he should have honourd, God, and evinced sufficient anxiety for his own soul, by comparing the penny books with the "word of truth." Rome prints and publishes devotional books and legends, suited to every mind, nation and people. A collection of outrageous or blasphemous penny books could be bound up for a few shillings that would surprise every English-man who has not been blinded by the Tractarian or by the Roman Priests. It is not very long since we purchased the following "Narrative" for 5 cents, within 60 miles of Rome. It is surmounted, by a rude wood-cut, very accurately re-produced on the title page. The reader may rest assured that the contents of the "Narrative" are *not exceptionally* outrageous, and that a thousand similar papers could be collected in Italy or France, a thousand times worse. It was probably written by some half educated priest, as the style is much encumbered, ungrammatical throughout, and in one or two places, obscure. The original has been left with the printer where the reader may call to see it, if he has any curiosity for such things.

RELATION
Of our Lord jesus Christ
To the Sisters, Elizabeth, Martha, and Brigit, desirous of knowing some particulars of His Passion, and after they had prayed, He appeard unto them, and said,

In the first place, be it known unto you my Sisters, that I received 112 blows in the face, and 3 blows with clenched fist, on the mouth; from the garden where I was seized, up to Ann's house, I fell 7 times, and was knocked down 105 times; I received 180 strokes on my back, and on my legs, received 32 contusions; I was lifted up by the hair and beard 32 times, and received a mortal blow; at the Column I received 6666 strokes, emitted 126 sighs, and was drawn and dragged along the ground, 33 times; on my Head I had 100 punctured wounds; on the Cross I received 3 mortal concussions; I was spat on the face 32 times; they inflicted 1000 sores on me; the number of the Soldiers who seized me, was 303, those who led me bound with cords, were 3, and the drops of blood which I shed were 38514.

Unto those who shall repeat seven "Pater" and seven "Ave" every day for the space of 23 years and 12 days, according to the number of the drops of my blood, I will grant seven favors on behalf of their soul.

First. I will grant him plenary indulgence and remission of all his sins.

Second. He shall not suffer the pains of purgatory
Third.   Should he die before the above stated time,
         I will grant him the same favors as if he
         had lived to accomplished it.
Forth.   I will reward him, as though he had been
         a martyr, and shed his blood for the faith.
Fifth.   I will descend from heaven to earth in the
         hour of his death, to receive his soul in my
         arms, and the souls of all those of his house,
       · and of his kindred to the forth remove; and
         if they shall be in Purgatory, I will convey
         them to enjoy the celestial country of life
         eternal.

This Relation was found in the Holy Sepulchre of
Jesus Christ our Lord, and whosoever will carry it on
his person, shall be free from the devil, sudden death,
and from other violent deaths, and if a pregnant woman shall wear it on her person, she shall have an
excellent delivery; and in those houses wherein this
Relation is kept, no evil shall come, and whosoever
shall wear it on his person 40 days before his death,
shall by *grace, see the glorious* Virgin Mary. Amen.

*Of how profitable it is to pity the Virgin Mary for
the five greater sorrows, which she suffered in this life.*
As a certain holy Father was once praying, he heard
Jesus Christ ask of his most holy Mother, which, and
how many had been the greatest sorrows which she
suffered in this life, and she replied in this wise:
Five Among others, were the greater sorrows which
I experienced, while living on the Earth.
First.   when Simeon predicted to me that thou
         shouldest be slain.
Second. When I thought thee lost, and when I
sought for thee three days.

Third. When I heard that thou hadst been taken and bound.

Fourth. When I saw thee again on the Cross.

Fifth. When I saw thee in the Sepulchre.

And Jesus Christ replied saying, know my Mother that whosoever shall, in remembrance of thy first sorrow, salute thee by repeating a " Pater " or an "Ave," the same shall obtain from me the remission of his transgressions. Whosoever will do the same, in respect of thy third, shall receive from me all those virtues which he lost on account of sin.

Whosoever will do the same, in respect of thy fourth, I will vouchsafe unto him the gift of my grace, and I will give him my body for meat, before he dies.

Whosoever will do the same, in respect of thy fifth, I will appear unto him when he dies, and will make him heir of eternal life Amen.

ADVERTISMENT.

Reflect, O Christian Soul on the persons to whom the above Relation was revealed, and that no one can acquire any indulgence, if the Soul is not in the grace of God.

Ferrara and Bassano (with permission of the Superiors.)

The above, like thousands of similar productions, are *far* beyond anything to which the following Scripture can apply:

"Not giving heed," said the inspired Apostle, " to jewish fables, and commandments of men, that turn from the truth." Titus 1. 14

At p. 317 Dr. Newman alludes to the gift, from the Dr. Russell, of St. Alfonso Liguori's sermons. Finding nothing about " Mariolatry" in the sermons, he wrote to the President, "to ask whether any thing had been left out in the translation. The reply was that "there certainly was an omission of one passage about the

p. 313. Blessed Virgin." Now everybody, whether "Catholic" or "Protestant" would at once have accepted this, as one of a thousand proofs that Rome suits herself to every era, and to every people. The "omission" was of course, made for English readers, and English difficulties. Dr. Newman however, with his curiously deceived mind, adds the following remark— "This omission, in the case of a book intended for Catholics, at least showed that such passages as are found in the works of Italian authors, were not acceptable to every part of the Catholic World. Such devotional manifestations in honor of our Lady had been my great *crux* as regards Catholisism,; I say frankly, I do not fully enter into them now; I trust I do not love her the less, because I cannot enter into them. They may be fully explained and defined; but sentiment and taste do not run with logic. They are suited for Italy, but they are not suited for p. 318. England." This last sentence is very likely to engender a feeling of contempt, even in those who desire to repress this sentiment. As Dr. Newman however, has spoken of a translation, of the Italian Saint(!), in which an omission is made touching Mary, it is proper that we should here expose the bold effrontery and deliberate wickedness of the Roman priesthood by placing before the public, a few extracts from another book by the same Roman Catholic saint. Other systems, such as the Braminical and the Mahometan &c. have indeed, most lamentably based error upon error, or substituted error for error. But Rome, has, for fifteen hundred years, Romans 1. 25 striven to "change the *truth* of God into a lie."

The following extracts are from Liguori's "Glories of Mary," sold by J.J. Wallwork, Great Malborough Street, and thus authorized by Cardinal Wiseman:—

"We hereby approve of the translation of 'THE

GLORIES OF MARY,' and cordially recommend it to the Faithful."

NICHOLAS CARD. WISEMAN,

Given at Westminster, on the Feast of Saint Alphonsus de Liguori, A.D.1852

ARCHBISHOP OF WESTMINSTER.

LIGUORI.

"Mary so loved the world as to give her only begotten Son."— P. 449.

"If Mary is for us, who shall be against us?" P. 71.

"This Great virgin, who is the Mother of your God and Judge, is also the Advocate of the whole human race: fit for this office, for she can do what she will with God; most wise for she knows all the means of appeasing Him; universal for she welcomes all, and refuses to defend no one." P. 161.
"Go to Mary." . . . . . . "Our salvation is in her hands." . . . .
"He who is protected by Mary will be saved; he who is not, will be lost."—P. 136.

"Hail thou who art oppointed umpire between God and men." . . . . . "Hail reconciler of the whole world."—P. 245.

Ch. II. Sec. 1. *Mary is our Life, because she obtains us the pardon of our sins.*" In this section it is also said "with reason does an ancient writer call her 'the only hope of sinners' for by her help alone can we hope for the remission of our sins."

THE SCRIPTURES.

"GOD so loved the world, that HE gave his only begotten Son, that whosoever believeth in him should not perish, but have eternal life." John iii. 16.

"If GOD be for us, who can be against us;" *Rom.* viii. 31.

"We have an advocate with the Father, JESUS CHRIST, the righteous. 1 *John* ii-1.
"Him that cometh unto me I will in no wise cast him out." *John* vi 37
Jesus said, "Come unto Me." *Matt.* xi. 28.
"I AM THE WAY, the truth, and the life: no man cometh unto the Father, but by ME." *John* xiv. 6.
"By the name of JESUS CHRIST OF NAZARETH.........
neither is there salvation in any other: for there is no other name under heaven given amongst men, whereby we must be saved." *Acts* iv. 10--12.
"There is ONE GOD, and ONE MEDIATOR between God and men, the MAN CHRIST JESUS." 1 *Tim.* ii. 5.
"Wherefore it behoves HIM to be made like unto his brethren, that he might be MERCIFUL and FAITHFUL HIGH PRIEST in things pertaining to God, to MAKE RECONCILIATION for the sins of the people." *Heb.* ii. 17.
"When CHRIST, WHO IS OUR LIFE, shall appear." *Col.* iii. 4.
"As God' FOR CHRIST'S SAKE, hath forgiven you." *Eph.* iv. 32.

LIGUORI.

Sec. 9. "Mary renders death sweet to her clients."

Ch. III. Sec. 1. In heaven *Mary is the hope of* all."

Sec. 2. "Mary is the hope of sinners."

Sec. 3. "Mary is the peace maker between sinners and God."

Ch. VIII. Sec. 1. "Mary delivers her clients from Hell."

THE SCRIPTURES.

" The sting of death is sin ; and the strength of sin is the law. But thanks be to God, which giveth us the victory through our LORD JESUS CHRIST." 1 *Cor.* xv. 56. 57.

"God our Saviour, and Lord Jesus Christ, which is our hope." 1 *Tim.* i. 1.

" He is our peace . . . . that HE might reconcile both unto God in one body by the cross, having slain the enmity thereby ; and came and preached peace to you which were afar off." *Eph.* ii. 14—17.

" Ye turned to God from idols to serve the living and true God ; and to wait for his Son from heaven, whom he raised from the dead, even JESUS, WHICH DELIV. ERED US FROM THE WRATH TO COME." 1 *Thess.* i. 9.—16.

The following extracts are from the translation of "The Psalter of St. Bonaventura."

"Lady, thou hast searched me and thou hast known me; thou hast known my ruin and my disobedience."

" From the horrible torments of Hell, deliver us, O Lady."

"Have pity on me O Lady thou who art called the mother of mercy; and by the depth of thy mercy purify me from all mine iniquities."

"Let Mary arise and let her enemies be scattered; let them all be crushed beneath her feet."

"A profound peace is the lot of those who love thee, O Lady. their souls shall never see eternal death."

"O LORD THOU hast searched me, and known me." *Psalm* cxxxix. 1.

"Thy vows are upon me, O GOD; I will render praises unto Thee FOR THOU HAST DE. LIVERED MY SOUL FROM DEATH." *Psalm* lvi. 12. 13.

" Have mercy upon me, O GOD, according to thy lovingkindness : according unto the multitude of thy tender mercies, blot out my transgressions. Wash me throughly from mine iniquity, and cleanse me from my sin." *Ps.* li. 1. 2.

" Let GOD ARISE, let his enemies be scattered : let them also that hate him flee before him." *Ps.* lxviii. 1.

"THOU wilt keep him in perfect peace whoso mind is stayed on thee : because he trusteth in THEE." *Isaiah* xxvi. 3, 4.

"Jesus said, I am the resurrection, and the life ; he that believeth in Me, though he were dead, yet shall he live." *John* xi. 25, 26.

LIGUORI.	THE SCRIPTURES.

LIGUORI.

"Save me O Lady, because the waters of lust have risen to my soul."

"He who dwells in the confidence of the mother of God, shall abide under her protection."

"Come let us celebrate our Lady, let us sing the Virgin Queen, our Salvation."

"The Lord is the God of vengeance; but thou, the benign mother of mercy, thou wilt turn him to pity."

"Thou, Lady, thou hast saved my soul."

"Sing unto our Lady a new Canticle, because she has done marvels."

"Blessed is the man who fears our Lady, and blessed is the heart that cherisheth her."

"Children, praise the Mother of God: old men, glorify her name."

THE SCRIPTURES.

"Save me O GOD; for the waters are come in unto my soul." *Psalm* lxix. 1.

"He that dwelleth in the secret place of THE MOST HIGH shall abide under the shadow of THE ALMIGHTY," *Psalm* xci' 11

"Come let us sing UNTO THE LORD; let us make a joyful noise to the rock of our salvation." *Ps.* xcv. 1.

"Who is a God like unto thee, that pardoneth iniquity, He . . . delighteth in mercy." *Mic* vii. 18.

"God commendeth His love towards us, in that, while we were yet sinners, Christ died for us. Being now justified by His blood, we shall be saved from wrath, through HIM." *Rom* v. 8, 9.

"As I live, saith the Lord God, I have no pleasure in the death of the wicked; but that the wicked turn from his way and live." *Ezekiel* xxxiii. 11.

"A just God and a Saviour; there is none beside MF. Look unto ME, and be saved, all the ends of the earth: for I am God, and there is none else." *Isaiah* xlv. 21, 22'

"O sing UNTO THE LORD a new song . . . . . Declare HIS WONDERS among all the people." *Psalm* xcvi. 1—3.

"Blessed is the man that trusteth in the LORD, and whose hope the LORD is." *Jer* xvii. 7.

"Both young men and maidens; old men and children . let them praise the NAME OF THE LORD: for his name alone is excellent." *Psalm* cxlviii. 12, 13.

The affair of the Jerusalem Bishopric shocked and broke Dr. Newman's allegiance to the English Establishment. But the above mixture of indecency, folly and fearful sin against the Holy Ghost, does not shock or shake him. St. Peter, of whom Rome boasts so

much, declared that *No* prophecy of the Scripture is of
any private interpretation. "Brethren" said St. Paul,
"I speak after the manner of man; Though it be a *man's*
testament, yet if it be confirmed, *no man disannuleth*
or *addeth* thereto." But Dr. Newman has no scruples
in setting God's Testament at defiance, and in up-
holding the system that canonizes a set of men, who
boldly and deliberately sin against the Spirit, by perverting "the Scriptures of truth." And after perverting
the word of God, in order to impose some new "definition," of which the above is only one specimen, Dr.
Newman assures us, that in accepting and believing it,
we are only "holding what the Apostles held before
us"! Truly the Romish priesthood, are, in the worst
sense, a "law unto themselves." The religious system they have now built, and packed up, is similar
to, but *worse* than the worship of the Babylonian Col-
ony in Samaria. "They feared the Lord, and served
their own gods."

In some part of his Apology, Dr. Newman tells us
that he could hardly say what his feelings would be,
if he were to witness an "Act of Faith." We do not
think the public take any interest, as to what his feelings
might, or might not be, on beholding such a fiendish
proceeding. But has he nothing to say about the crimes
committed, and the blood shed, by the Priests of Rome?
No religious system has saturated its altars with as
much blood as the Roman. The Inquisition alone, since
its foundation in the 14th century, has burnt at the
stake, above 100,000 persons of both sexes, besides
destroying twice that number by imprisonment, and
exclusive of open slaughter, as on the eve of St. Bartho-
lemew, when 7000 were killed. When the Spaniards
landed in America, the Pope was of course anxious
that that Continent also, should acknowledge his

p. 393.

spiritual dominion. Excited by the Jesuits, and by the desire to get at the inexhaustible treasures the Natives were supposed to possess, the Spaniards, altho received with reverence and hospitality, conducted themselves with the most shocking cruelty. The rack, the scourge, and the faggot were employed to convert them to Chrisianity! They were hunted down like wild beasts, or burnt in their thickets and fastness. When Diego d'Almagro, and Francis Pizaro landed in Peru, the first thing they did, was to require the reigning monarch to embrace " Christianity," and to surrender all his dominions to Charles V. who had obtained them as a gift from the Pope! On some demur taking place, the Spaniards, true to their Roman Catholic Christianity, massacred 5000 of the Peruvians, and strangled their monarch at a stake. Unparalleled however, as are the crimes of the Romish Priests, surprising as its subtle deceit and love of darkness is, far more astonishing is it, that mankind have borne with this system for so many centuries, and that some who were not brought up under its dominion, but who have oft times listened to the word of God from their earliest days, should be so easily inthraled by it, and get to learn the depths of Satan.

Before many years have passed however, we shall all, with Dr. Newman and his teachers, stand before God, when " the Judgement shall be set, and the books opened." How many alas ! shall appear, who were once laden with " the traditions, the commandments and doctrines of men ; " who hoped in " a sacramental system ; a principle of developement"; a sojourn in a Purgatory, in the worship of images, intercession of saints, but who nevertheless died in their sins. Dan. vii. 10 Col. 11. 8. 22.

But many readers will now exclaim . . . ' How can all this do Dr. Newman any good ? No soul can be argued into the new birth, and "the natural man *cannot* discern the spiritual things of God." It is not plain that he "hath been ever learning and hath never been able to come to the knowledge of the truth"? Our reply is : that this is perfectly , we had almost said, too true, and it is in the *earnest* and *prayerful* hope that Dr. Newman and many others may open their eyes to the truth as it is in *Jesus,* that we now conclude with a brief exposition of the Gospel, as set forth by the Redeemer himself, and as preached by his Apostles.*

No one more than Dr. Newman, admits the stringency of the simple, yet comprehensive truth enunciated by the Saviour himself . . . . "Marvel not John iii. 7. that I say unto thee ye must be born again." I will turn away therefore, from the latent, and scientific infidelity, that is getting so common in this country, and which pervades the rest of Europe. Neither will I speak of the liberalism of many who believe that they live, and let live, but are dead. I will start from *the* fundamental truth, ye must be born again," and if Dr. Newman will accept that which God hath plainly revealed, respecting the attainment of the new birth, he shall perceive how Satan hath hitherto, corrupted his mind 2 Cor. xi. 3. from the simplicity that is in Christ."

In the xv of the first Epistle to the Corinthians, the Apostle speaks of two distinct persons or heads; Of the *first* man Adam— and of the *second* man, the Lord from heaven. Both are there set before us and contrasted, and I request the reader with his mind's eye, to keep them distinctly before him.

---

* Rome, and all who imitate Rome, go about the world preaching a "Church" and a faith based on some special Creed, or Articles. But the commandment of the Lord to the Apostles was simply . . . Go ye into all the world, and preach the *gospel* to every creature." Neither do we any where read of St. Paul and the other Apostles, preaching a particular system of theology. They preached Christ delivered for our offences and risen again for our justification.

Now "as is the earthly," says the apostle, such are they also that are earthly," and as decendants, and offspring of the first man Adam, we are *by nature,* 1. Cor. xv.48. after his likeness, fallen from grace, corrupt, and "sold under sin." Proceeding as we do, from one common, corrupt, and sinful stock, *we are,* as the apostle said to the Ephesians, " by nature children of wrath." And not only are we, as children of Adam, "alienated from Eph. iv. 18. the life of God" but " alienated and enemies in our Col. 1. 21. *mind, by wicked works."* In this state we are " lost," and unless redeemed, we shall *certainly* fall short of the kingdom of heaven.

But if we may be cut off, as it were, and *altogether* removed from our evil origin, and be transformed and engrafted *in* the *second* Adam, the holy and undefiled Lord from heaven, then we shall no longer belong to a sinful, but to a holy stem; we shall then proceed from, and form part of the pure and holy body of the *second* man, the Lord Jesus Christ, and be *new* creatures *in him.* For if any man be *in* "Christ" saith the Scriptures, "he is a *new* creature." It is plain that I *must* be a new creature, if I become a member of the body of Christ.

Now the end for which the Son of God came into the World, was to sever us, and remove us from the first and sinful man Adam, who was the figure of Him that was to come," and ingraft us *in* Himself. Rom. v. 14.

Let Dr. Newman then bear in mind this; that the end for which Christ, the Son of God came into the World, to die, and to rise again from the dead, was to sever us from the first, sinful and corrupt Adamic nature, and to re-create us *in* Himself, the second Adam, and Lord from heaven, and thus makes us partakers of his own divine nature.

Now it is easy for us sinners, to percieve, and to understand the way in which, all who submit to be taught of God, may, by His power, be endowed with the *new birth*, free of taint and sin. It is easy, we repeat, to apprehend what the Scriptures mean, by declaring, that "as many as receive Christ, to them gave he power to become the *Sons of God*, even to them that *believe* on his name." We cannot become Sons of God without being born again. And born, not of *blood*, nor of the John 1.12, 13 *flesh*, nor of the *will of man*, but *of God*." No verse in the Word is more exclusive and conclusive than this one. We must be born again, and that birth must be *of God*.

But we must first *die* before we can rise again, regenerated, and in possession of the new birth, or new life. We must *first* get rid of our old, evil, and sinful Adamic nature, before we can be re-created, by a new birth, that shall be *of God*. And the reader must not think that this is to be accomplished by natural death in the course of nature, but that this death, and this new birth, whereof we speak, was accomplished for him eighteen hundred years ago, when the Lord Jesus Christ died, and rose again. To attain unto this *saving* knowledge, the reader is to bear in mind, that *all*, in him, that pertained, and which he, by nature inherited, from the first Adam, was judged, crucified, and put *to death, in* the second Adam, the Redeemer, Jesus Christ, when He died on the Cross. When therefore, with the eye of my understanding and faith, I look at Christ, nailed to the Cross, and raised up on high, as Moses lifted up the serpent in the wilderness, then and there, I see *in* Christ the *second* Adam, my *whole evil nature*, called in the Scriptures, "*the old man*," receive its *death* blow. "*Our old man*" said the Rom. vi 6. apostle, "has been Crucified *with* Christ, that the *body of sin* might be *destroyed.*" The Son of God came "*in the likeness of sinful flesh,*" and was *made sin* that he might, "*his ownself,* bear *our* sin in his own body, on the Cross." The first truth we have to understand, is that our old, evil, and disgraced nature, was laid on the Redeemer, and was crucified and put to death *in* Him. "I have been Crucified," said St. Paul, "*with* Christ." [1 Pet. ii. 24.] [Gal: ii. 20]

Our old nature having thus died, we are 'everlastingly endowed with a *new birth* by being *united,* and made *one with Christ* when he rose from the grave and became the *first begotten* of the dead. "For if" saith the Scriptures, "we have been planted *together,* in the likeness of His *death,* we shall be also in the likeness of his *resurrection.*" If the reader therefore will look back 1800 years, and contemplate the opening of the grave of Christ, and behold Him rising forth into life, and believe that by the power of God, he, the reader, shares that resurrection and that new life *in,* and *with* Christ, then he shall perceive and understand how by the *resurrection* of Christ, he is *born again.* And born again not of blood, nor of the will of the flesh, nor of the will of man, but *born of God.* In this way, my old self and nature, which pertained to and proceeded from the first man Adam, was *destroyed* in *Christ* in his death; but by union with Him in His *resurrection,* I have been for ever ingrafted in Him, the second man, and Lord from heaven. We now understand the wonderful meaning of the apostle's exclamation—"Blessed be the God and Father of our Lord Jesus Christ, which according to his abundant mercy hath *begotten us again,* unto a *living* hope by the *resurrection* of Christ from the *dead.*" For "God's *great love,* wherewith he loved us, even when we were *dead* in sins, HATH *quickened* us *together* WITH Christ, and HATH *raised* us up to- [Rev: i. 5.] [Rom. vi. 5.] [1. Pet. 1. 3.] [Eph. ii 4.5.6] *gether* IN Christ." In Him we are born again, and as bone of *his* bone, and flesh of *his* flesh, we are made *partakers* of *the divine nature* "I in *them,* and thou in *me,* that *they* may be made perfect *in one."*

2 Pet 1; 4
John xvii.23.

The reader may now see, why and how, "to as many as receive Christ, to them gave he power to become the *Sons of God.* even to them that *believe* on his name." It says *believe* in his name, because *nothing* that we can do, could unite us to the Lord Jesus Christ, either in his death or in his resurrection. But if we *believe* on his name, saith the Scripture, he giveth us *power* to become sons of God. Our simple bare belief, does not do this, but the *truth* we believe in, concerning the son of God, *does.* And we become sons of God, because as He is the Son of God, and as we are *one with Him,* bone of his bone and flesh of his flesh, so therefore must we also be, *in him,* Sons of God. This is the meaning, and this is the simple reason, or rather cause, why "we are all the children of God, *by faith in Christ Jesus."* Because we know and believe, that "when the fulness of the time was come, God sent forth his Son, made of a woman, made under the law, to redeem them that were under the law, that we might receive the *adoption of sons.* "Behold," exclaims the apostle, with great emphasis," what *manner* of love the Father hath bestowed upon us, that we should be called the *sons* of God! Beloved *now* are we the sons of God, and it doth not yet *appear* what we shall be: but we know that when *he* shall appear we shall be *like him* for we shall see him as he is. And

1 John iii.1.

because ye *are* sons, God hath sent forth the spirit of his Son into your hearts, crying Abba Father. Wherefore, says this Scripture, "thou art no more a servant, but a *Son,* and if a son, then an *heir* of God, through Christ."

Gal: iv.4.—7

"We are heirs of God," because, inasmuch as He hath

constituted His Son heir of all things, and as we also are His sons, it follows that we shall be co-heirs together with the Son of God. And the Scripture says *"through Christ,"* because we can only be begotten again and be sons and heirs of God, *through Christ,* and not by anything we could ourselves do.

The new birth is not therefore, a partial one, but as complete, as a death and a resurrection could make it; and to be in, and of Christ, is to be *wholly* and *permanently* saved. The reader may *now* fully understand and rely, on the words of the Lord Jesus Christ, so often repeated, and so often varied, inviting all to come, and *believe* in him, for redemption and salvation.

"He that *believeth* in me shall not come unto condemnation, but *is* passed from *death* unto *life."* John v. 24.

" The blood of Jesus Christ cleanseth us from all sin." "The blood is the life," and laden with our sins, he yielded up that life, " the just *for* the unjust." 1. John 1. 7.

"God so loved the world, that he gave his only begotten Son, that whosoever *believeth* in him, should *not* perish, but have *everlasting* life.

"For God sent not his Son into the world to condemn the world; but that the world *through him* might be saved."

"He that *believeth* on him, *is not* condemned: but he that believeth not, is condemned *already,* because he hath *not believed* in the name of the only begotten Son of God;" as many thousands do, who are carried away and spoiled with divers doctrines, " through philosophy and vain deceit, after the tradition of *men,* after the elements of the *world,* and *not* after Christ," John iii. 16—18. Col. 11. 8. Heb. xiii. 9.

On one occasion, they asked Christ, saying, "what shall we *do* that *we* may *work* the works of God." The Lord's answer was :

36

"This is the work *of God*, that ye *believe* in him whom
_{John vi. 29.} he hath sent."

The reader, and we trust Dr. Newman also, will now
perceive why eternal life is spoken of as a free *gift*,
and not as a reward. For not only did the Father in his
love for a fallen world, *give* his only begotten son as
a ransom, but nothing that we can do, can have *any*
part or share in the redemption wrought by the death
and resurrection of our substitute Jesus Christ. "The
gift of God," wrote the Apostle, to the *Romans*, "is
_{Rom. vi. 23.} *eternal* life through Jesus Christ our Lord." "And to
him that worketh *not*, but *believeth* on him that justi-
_{Rom. iv. 5.} fieth the ungodly, his *faith* is counted *for* righteous-
ness." Further on, in the same Epistle, the Apostle
speaks much more fully of freedom from sin, of justification, of righteousness, and of eternal life, as a *gift*.

Contrasting sin and its consequences, in the first
Adam, with the redeeming sacrifice of Christ, St. Paul
shows that it is easy to perceive, that if condemnation
and death came by the one man, Adam, it is not a hard
thing to perceive that the sacrifice of the man Jesus
Christ, much *more* than neutralized and atoned, for the
transgression of the first Adam, and for ours.

"But not, he says, as the *act of transgression*, so
also is the *gift* of grace; because if by the transgression
of the man Adam, the many have died, *much more*, did
the *grace* of God, and the *gift abound*, in the grace of
the one man Jesus Christ, towards the *many*." So much
for the free *grace* and *gift* that *exacted nothing*, and
exceeded in measure and in degree, that which a righteous and just God might have required of his disobedient
creatures.

But we are not only redeemed, we are also justified;
For "not as by *one* having sinned, *so* is the *gift*; because

the judgment was by *one* to condemnation, but the *free gift* by *grace*, is of *many* offences unto *justification*." The Lord Jesus Christ, not only atoned for the one sin of Adam, sometimes called original sin, but he wrought for us a free remission of *many* offences, and *justified* us. The Queen of these realms, might be pleased to grant me a free pardon for a crime committed by me, either against the law, or against her person; but she could not dismiss me from her presence a *righteous* man, as well as a pardoned one. And even a pardoned culprit is not free of the *guilt* of his crime. But it is otherwise with God, towards those of his fallen creatures, who take Him at his word. Thus all who perceive and believe, that the Sacrifice of His Son freed them from all sin, are not only pardoned, but free of guilt, and *righteous*; not righteous of themselves but *in* Christ. "For He hath made Christ who knew no sin, sin for us, that we might be made the *righteousness of God*, in him."

2 Cor. v. 21.

But he did more than all this. We needed more than remission of sins and righteousness. We needed *life*, and he came to give us *life*, and life eternal. "For if by the offence of one man, *death reigned* by one; *much more* they which receive *abundance* of grace, and the *gift* of *righteousness*, reign *in life* by the one Jesus Christ," " Therefore," concludes the Apostle, " as by means of *one* transgression, it came upon *all men* unto condemnation, *even so* by one *righteous* act, it came upon all men unto *justification*, for as by one man's disobedience the many were made sinners, so also by the obedience of *one man*, the *many* be *made righteous*."

Rom v. 15.
to end

Yea, even more than all this. As members of the holy body of our Lord and Redeemer, we are not only righteous, but *sanctified*; purified and *"renewed* in the *spirit of our mind,"* so that we can have perfect fellowship with the *holiness of God.* This attribute, like every other, we cannot of ourselves acquire, but we are *sanctified* through "the offering of the body of Jesus Christ once for all. For both he that *Sanctifieth*, and they that *are Sanctified*, are all *one*: for which cause he is not ashamed to call them *brethren.*

Heb. x. 10.

Heb. ii. 11.

For Dr. Newman's sake, and for the Reader's, be he "Catholic" or "Protestant." the following short recaptitulation is now added, which it is believed, will in a measure, unfold the depths of that truth declared by the Spirit, that—It pleased the Father that in him, Christ, should all fulness dwell," and show moreover, that "of His *fulness,* have all we received, and grace for grace."

Col. 1. 19

John 1. 16.

First.

When *dead* in trespasses and sin—twice dead, as it were, because we have not kept, but broken the *law,* —without strength to save our soul, "Christ bore our sin in his own body on the tree, and died *for* the *ungodly,* blotting out the hand writing of *ordinances* that was against us, which was *contrary* to us, and took it out of the way, nailing it to the cross. In this was manifested the love of God towards us that He sent his only-begotten son into the World, that we might *live* through him."

Eph. ii. 1

Gal. iii. 10.

Rom. v.6–8

Eph. 11. 15.

Col. 11. 14.

1 John iv. 9.

Second.

Those therefore who were once children of *wrath* and *enemies,* He hath now *reconciled* to himself by *Jesus Christ* in the body of his flesh, through *death,* to present us holy and unblameable and unreproveable in His sight.

Eph. 11. 3.

2 Cor. v. 18.

Col: 1.20—22

Third.

Hence it is that since "faith came," the God of Heaven calls upon us, in his *grace*—to *trust,* to put our *faith* in, to *believe,* that because his only beloved

Son was made sin *for* us, and suffered *for* us, He is 2 Cor. v 18—20.
now reconciled unto us, not imputing our trespasses
unto us. *Faith* therefore that *depends*, and *relies*, on
the atonement of Christ, is faith that saves. And John xx. 31.
this is what is meant by such Scriptures as :—

"A man is justified by *faith.*" Rom. iii. 28.

" By grace ye are saved, through *faith.*" Eph. 2. 8.

"From a child thou hast known the holy Scriptures,
which are able so make thee wise unto salvation,
through *faith*, which is in Jesus Christ," 2 Tim. iii. 15

"*Believe* in the Lord Jesus Christ, and thou shalt
be saved."
Acts xvi. 31.

"If ye *believe* not that I am he, ye shall die in your
sins."
John viii. 24

If we are saved by faith in God's only begotten son, *Fourth.*
who *gave* himself for our sins, then salvation and life
everlasting, is a gift:—

"If thou knewest;" said the Redeemer, "if thou knewest the *gift* of God, and who it is that saith unto thee,
give me to drink, thou wouldest have asked of *him*,
and *he* would have *given* thee living water." John iv. 10.

The life that believers have, being *life in Christ*, it *Fifth.*
must follow therefore, that the gift whereof we speak,
cannot be temporal, or for a time, but *eternal.* "I have
been crucified with Christ," said St. Paul; "nevertheless I live; yet not I, but *Christ* liveth *in me*: and Gal. ii. 20
the life which I now live in the flesh, I live by the faith
of the Son of God." On which truth the following
Scriptures are of course, based.

"I *give* unto them *eternal* life, and they shall *never
perish*, neither shall any pluck them out of my hand." John x. 28.

"This is the promise that he hath promised us,
1 John ii. 25. even *eternal* life."

"The wages of sin is *death,* but the *gift* of God is
Rom. vi. 23. *eternal* life, through Jesus Christ our Lord."

"Neither by the blood of goats and calves, but by
his own blood, he entered in once, into the holy place,
Heb. ix. 12. having obtained *eternal* redemption."

Sixth.   Now it is these truths that constitute our peace; a
present, perfect, and imperturable peace. All doubt is
excluded. The spirit that may have had torment,
sadness, and even anguish, because of sin, death, and
judgment, may *now* rest in the full assurance of being
at peace with God.

"Being justified by faith," wrote St. Paul to the
Romans, we have *peace* with God *through our Lord*
Rom. v. 1 *Jesus Christ.*"

"But now *in* Christ Jesus, ye who sometimes were
far off, are made nigh by the blood of Christ, for *he*
Eph. ii. 13.14 is our *peace,*"

"*Peace* I leave with you, *my* peace I *give* unto you:
not as the world giveth, give I unto you. Let not
John xiv. 27. your heart be troubled, neither let it be afraid."

Seventh.   Finally, The following Scripture mention one more
attribute which pertains to the redeemed, even their
Sanctification.

"For of him are ye, *in Christ Jesus,* who *of God* is
made unto us, wisdom, and righteousness, and *Sanc-*
1 Cor. i 30.
vi 11. *tification* and redemption."

The word is always "*in* him," *in Christ Jesus,*
because we cannot acquire any of these things
ourselves.

The reader, we trust, will now apprehend the fulness and comfort of the Apostle's words to the Colossians:

"Ye are *complete* in him." Col: II. 10.

And in a measure also, the depth of the Redeemer's declaration to the Father:

"I have *finished* the work which thou gavest me to do." John xvii. .4

Now to Dr. Newman and to many others, this gospel is foolishness.

The God of Heaven, does, in his grace, lead his children, *scattered among all nations and people,* unto some particular truth, or order of truth recorded and developed in His word, according to their need, danger or trials. But Dr. Newman, and many others, believe and hope in a human theory, called the Theory of Developement, by which it is assumed, that God's Old and New Testament is not all that He had to reveal unto mankind, but that His will is, that a set of men in the city of Rome, with the Pope at their head, should develope new truths, new ideas, and new definitions. Thus they have at various periods, ordered Auricular Confession.— Indulgences—Absolution— The Real Presence in a Wafer— Prayers for the dead—Patron Saints—Works of Supererogation, and Roman Infallability. The last "definition" being the immaculate conception of Mary, entitling her Queen of Heaven. and virtually adding a goddess to the Holy Trinity.*

---

* The intention of this recent " definition " respecting Mary, is to introduce the Female element into the Romish worship. The nature, and early preservation of both brute and human life, is entirely dependant on the Female, whose love and instinct is fine, and acute, in behalf of their young; while the offspring, on their part, readily depend on Maternal love, Maternal indulgence, and Maternal sympathy. This natural and reciprocal instinct, Rome has personified by a goddess; borrowing the expedient, from antient mythology. Thus Mary, has, in our generation, taken the place of Isis, Ashteroth, Venus, &c. of various heathen nations, and Saraswati of the Hindoos. This introduction of female instinct and sympathy into the Romish system, helps both to consolidate, and support it, because it finds a ready and early response in the heart and feeling of many, and especially of school girls and young women. In France girls, and young ladies are very

"But," said the inspired Apostle to the Romans, " I find a law, that when I would do *good, evil* is present with me. For I delight in the law of God after the *inward* man, but I see *another* law in my *members*, warring against the law of my *mind*, and bringing me into captivity to the law of sin which is in my members." Thus altho' we are redeemed and righteous *in* Christ, our *mortal* body or flesh, is not better than it was, but just as bad. It is still literally, *prone* to sin, and always striving to delight itself in sin, worldliness, and selfwill. The "flesh lusteth against the *spirit*, and the spirit against the *flesh*, and these two are contrary to one another," and we are, especially if not watchful and prayerful, constantly liable to get defiled, both in thought, word, and deed. This terrible warfare commences with the New birth in Christ, and only ends with the death of the body.

Rom. vii. 21—23.

But our God and Father, who loved us before the foundation of the world, hath made ample and *perfect* provision for us, as he did for Israel. The first covenant had ordinances of divine service, and a worldly sanctuary. There the high Priest, was *continually* ministering before Jehovah, in behalf of His people. The children of Israel were the people of God, but they were, as we are, constantly falling into sin and uncleanness, and sometimes into unavoidable defilement. It was necessary therefore, that their High Priest should *constantly* minister before God, in their behalf; beside the

thoughtful, and full of pretty attentions to the image of Mary, in whom repose all their hope and sympathies. Now Rome declares that a man's destiny is formed on its mother's knees. In connection with this Roman, "definition," the general reader may peruse Bacon's *Wisdom of the Ancients;* and a delightful essay *on maternal love in nature,* by Schroeder Van derKolk ; Prof. at Utrecht. We believe the Essay has been translated into English. The Public in this country may rest assured that the English language does not possess a thorough Work on the philosophy of the Romish religion. No one can attempt to show what Romanism really is, except those who are acquainted with the inner life or rather experience, of an intelligent and sincere Roman Catholic. Probably the best definition of the system is, that— *It is man's lie based on God's truth.*

perpetual Morning and Evening sacrifice. The High
Priest stood between Jehovah and his people, and was
always intent, by sacrificial intercession, on keeping
Israel free of uncleanness, and defilement. Now those
things, and those ordinances, were but "a shadow of
good things *to come.*" They were *patterns* of things
in Heaven;" hence the Apostle writing to the He- Heb. x. 1.
brews saith, "Now of the things we have spoken, this
is the sum : we have such an HighPriest, who is set
on the right hand of the throne of the Majesty in
Heaven; a minister of the *true* tabernacle, which the
Lord pitched and not man. For Christ is not entered
into the holy places made with hands, which were the
figures of the true, but into heaven itself, *now* to
appear in the presence of God *for* us." No sooner do Heb. viii. 1.2.
his redeemed, sin or defile themselves, than the Son, ix. 24.
consecrated a high Priest for evermore, pleads and
interceds for them, and keeps them pure and fault-
less before his Father and their Father. "Therefore"
saith the Apostle, He is able to save them to the utter-
most, that come unto God *by him*, seeing he ever
liveth to make intercession for them." And "we have Heb. vii. 25.
not a High Priest, which *cannot* be touched with the
feeling of our infirmities; but one who was in *all*
points tried like as we are, yet without sin." Hence
the word is—"if any man sin he hath an advocate with
the Father, Jesus Christ the righteous. Let us therefore come *boldly* unto the throne of grace, that we
may obtain *mercy*, and find *grace* to help in *every*
time of need." Blessed assurance; glorious truth ! To Heb. iv.15.16
supplant which, Rome has commanded, Auricular
confession, Absolution, Penance, and decreed the existence of a *Purgatory*; and all in the name of the
Lord, whose everlasting Gospel it has turned into a
savour of death unto death. *

It is very important that the question of Works should not be passed over in silence, because it is one that many neglect, and almost as many misunderstand.

The first covenant that God made with man, is thus comprehensively summed up by the Apostle. "Moses describeth the righteousness which is of the *Law*. That the man which *doeth* those things shall *live* by them." The Law, and salvation by the Law, was not of *faith*. God revealed, clearly and concisely, the conditions on which he would accept man; declaring "that the man that *doeth* them, shall live in them." But so little have we been able to control our evil nature, and save our soul by obedience to the law of the ten commandments, that instead of being saved by the law, it is the law which proved our failure, and sealed our condemnation. The broken law, closes every mouth, and proves all the World guilty before God. The result being, that as many as are under the law, or who place themselves under the obligations of the law, as the Galatians did, "are under the *curse*: for it is written, "Cursed is every one that continueth not in *all* things which are written in the book of the law to do them." But here again 'our Redeemer and our substitute, thoroughly met our need, failure and guilt. He kept the whole law for us: and more than the whole law. "I do always, he himself declared, "those things which please Him." With the power, and claims of his own holiness and perfect obedience, " he redeemed us from the curse of the law, being made a curse *for* us: for it is written, cursed is every one that hangeth on a tree." And thus, as St. Paul

Gal. iii. 12.

Rom. iii. 19.

Gal: iii. 10.

Gal. iii. 13.

---

* The Priesthood of Christ is a truth that no Romanist, knows any thing about. We believe it is studiously ignored by Rome. To admit this truth, would of course, do away with two thirds and a half of its Priestly functions. The gift of the Holy Spirit to individual believers, is also quite ignored, even in theory.

said to the antient Romans, "Christ is the end of the law, for righteousness, to every one that *believeth.*" Rom. x. 4.10. "Therefore we conclude that by the deeds of the law, shall no man be justified in his sight, and that a man *is* justified by *faith*, without the deeds of the law." While dead in trespasses and sin, unable to deliver ourselves, Rom. iii. 20. through obedience to the ten commandments, the Lamb of God, willingly offered himself a sacrifice for us, and "was delivered for our offences, and rose again for our justification, that God might be the justifier of him that *believeth* in Jesus Christ." It is on this Rom. iii. 26. foundation that the Lord God has based his second testament or Covenant with mankind. The first was based on man's obedience to the law; The second is based on free grace.

But the New Testament, does, nevertheless, say a great deal about works; more perhaps than the Old Testament. With this difference: that under the first Covenant, our salvation depended on our obedience and observance of the law of works; whereas under the Second Covenant, a man is called unto good works when he *is* saved and because he is saved. In his Epistle to Titus, St. Paul puts this truth very plainly before us. Speaking of the second coming of Christ, the Apostle adds:—

" Who gave himself for us, that he might redeem us from *all* iniquity, and *purify* unto himself a *peculiar* people, *Zealous of good Works.*" All attempts Titus ii. 11. iii. 8. to serve God in any way, before, or unless we "are new creatures in Christ Jesus," is a delusion and a self-deception, as great, as it is common. If I am not in Christ, all my works, whatever they may cost me, are all dead works. The greatest abnegation of self, coupled with the utmost operative devotion, without the eternal union with Christ, is only a fatal attempt to offer unto God, the dead works of unclean hands. Let us all bear in mind, that it is not the *fruit* that does, or that can make the tree good; but it is the good *Tree* that bears good fruit. Hence, those only who are branches of the "true vine," can bear acceptable fruit. "Apart from me" saith the Redeemer, "ye can do nothing." There is another Scripture also, that speaks very plainly on this point. "By grace are ye saved, through *faith*, not of yourselves; it is the gift of God. Not of works, lest any man should boast, for we are *his* workmanship, created *in* Jesus Christ *unto good works*, which God hath before ordained that we should walk in them."

John xv.

Eph. ii. 8—10.

It is from the redeemed that God expects and accepts, obedience, love, and good works. There is no especial code for them. "Being made free from sin, they become *servants* of righteousness, *servants* of God." The precepts, the exhortations, the incentives to holiness, good works, and separation from the World, are so numerous and various in the New Testament, that it is not easy to classify, or to detail the privileges and responsibilities of the people of God. Thus the now scattered *members of Christ's body*, are exhorted :—

Rom. vi. 18. 22.

"As obedient *children*, not to fashion themselves according to their former lusts. Not to be conformed to this World," and to declare *plainly*, that they are not only pilgrims here, but that their *conversion*, has given them hopes, tastes, ideas of greatness and retributive justice &c, &c,, just the opposite to those they once professed, and which the World has established. As *holy and beloved in Christ*, they are exhorted to put on bowels of mercies, kindness, humbleness of

1. Pet. i. 14. Rom. xii. 2

mind, meekness. long-suffering, forbearance, and love, which is the bond of perfectness; and whatever they do in *word* or *deed*, to do *all* in the name of the Lord Jesus." Col. iii. 12.
to end.

Because they have *risen with Christ*, they are exhorted to seek those things that are above, and to mortify their body here below, and to have no confidence in the flesh. Col. iii. 1. 5.
Phi. iii. 3.

They are also exhorted to :—
Lay aside every weight, and the sin which doth so easily beset them, and to run the race set before them, with patience. Heb. xii. 1.

To be instant in prayer,
Fervent in spirit.
Rejoicing always in God.
To walk as becometh the Gospel of Christ.
To visit the fatherless and afflicted.
To pray for their enemies.
To be slow to speak, swift to hear.
To rejoice when afflicted and tried.
To present their bodies a living sacrifice, holy, acceptable unto God; and so on. Trusting to our memory, we may add, that there are precepts for Masters—precepts for servants—precepts for husbands, precepts for wives; exhortations to widows, old men, young men, children, fathers &c, and a comprehensive and general teaching, most blessed and profitable to those who turn to the Scriptures, as their daily spiritual food. Now as we have said before, a tree is always known by the fruit which it bears. A good tree will bear good fruit, even as one who is in Christ, will bear good fruit; some thirty, some sixty, and some a hundred fold. Heb. xii. 1.

If Abraham had not had a living faith, he *could not* have
offered up his Son Isaac upon the altar. But he showed
his *faith by his works*, and the Scripture was fulfilled
which saith, Abraham believed God, and it was im-
puted unto him for righteousness. Those who *are*
John x. 5. Christ's sheep, know his voice and follow him; and a
stranger *will they not follow*, but will *flee* from him.

But the Scriptures describe and warn us respecting
a numerous, and very powerful body, whose appearance in the world was nearly coeval with the first few
believers, and true disciples of Christ. The kingdom
of heaven, said the Lord, is likened unto a man which
sowed good seed in his field. The sower, we are told
was the Son of man himself; the Earth was his field,
and the good seed which he sowed, are the children
of the kingdom. But while men slept his enemy came
and sowed Tares among the wheat, and went his way.
Now the Tares ever represented as they do now, the
great and influential body we are about to speak of,
and recognized by the children of the kingdom, as
the great and powerful multitude of mere professors.
Like the Tares in the Parable, they spring, and con-
tinue to spring up, and to grow, side by side with the
good seed; learn the language, so to speak, of the
children of God; assume a similar form of faith, the
same hope, and the same responsibilities, and having
allied and fused themselves with the Secular Powers
have acquired a great and specious authority. They
are, nevertheless, as the Lord himself declared, not
the children of the kingdom, but the children of the
wicked one. They vary somewhat in character and
customs, as they belong to this or to that nation or
people, but they have certain invariable and prominent
features common to all, whether they be Romanist, or

Protestants, because they all own one common Romish origin. Their respective ecclesiastical establishments have steadily increased ever since they first began to germinate, it being Satan's object by means of this body to mar the distinctive character of the good seed, so that its heavenly origin should not be discerned; and he has amply succeeded. The secret of his success consisted and consists, in the specious way he leads the great body of mere professing christians, to base their deceptions, convictions, and ideas, on a subtile perversion of the *Word of God*. With idolators and others, Satan deals in other ways, but with the people of what are sometimes called christian nations, his aim has always been to turn the *light* into *darkness*, and so make the darkness very great. He first of all concentrated all his subtilty and power with the view of vitiating the simple and saving truth of the Gospel, that faith, that is hope, trust, and dependance on the sacrifice of the Son of God, wholly and perfectly redeems the sinner, not because faith redeems him, but because the atonement he *trusts* in, was both perfect and eternal. Half a century had scarcely elapsed however, and many were still living who had heard this truth from the Lord himself, when Satan, not by violent or by intollerant agents, but by "false brethren, unawares brought in," induced many to place themselves again under the yoke and the obligations of the Law and to believe that by fulfilling the same, they should be saved *through Christ*. Thus many were led and are led, to believe that the atonement was, as respects its intrinsic nature and purpose, complete and perfect, but that man is bound to make up for a certain measure of deficiency and unworthiness in himself, by his own individual efforts. In this way the love, the obedience, and the responsibilities of those who *are* saved, are complacently converted into auxilliaries, *conditional* to salvation. Ishmael, the son of the bond-woman, allegorically represents the bondage of those who were bound to the Covenant of the Law and of Works. Isaac, the child of promise, represents the second or present Covenant, which opens the kingdom of heaven to all *believers.* To admix and combine the old and new Covenants, and make a third one of his own, was, as we have said, Satan's first object; because by putting a piece of *new* cloth, to an *old* garment, the rent is made worse, even as that man's condition is worse than ever, who hopes to get rid of sin, not by either works or grace exclusively, but by works and grace combined. Nevertheless what saith the Scriptures? *"Cast out* the bond-woman and her son: for the Son of the bond-woman, *shall not be heir* with the Son of the free woman.'' But the Deceiver soon led many to decline saving grace; not by inducing religious persons utterly to ignore either grace or works, but by leading them to believe in a specious combination of the two, making, as it were, the son of the bond-women *co*-heir, with the son of the free, so that the sinner should not trust either in Works or in grace. Cain offered for himself the first-fruits of his own labour. But Abel, discerning by faith, the atonement that should be made by the Son of God, offered a spotless substitute, and was accepted. But the gospel believed and preached by the seed sown by "the enemy,'' consists in an altar, whereon the Lamb, together with man's works are placed and offered unto God, in the hope that both may prove sufficient. This first fundamental falsehood, flattering to the flesh and fatal to the soul, has never lost its hold of the great mass of mankind, and is the doctrine on which the Tares base their religious theories and systems. Thus teachers and preachers among them will proclaim :—

From first to last, salvation is the gift of God and that if we are justified it is of God's grace. True it is that we merit eternal life by our Works of obedience, not from their intrinsic worth, but from the free appointment and bountiful promise of God; and that we are able to do them at all, is the simple result of His grace. You depend upon God; but such admonitions imply also your dependence upon yourselves; for, did not your salvation, in some sufficient sense depend on yourselves, what would be the use of appealing to you not to forget your dependence on God. It is because you have so great a share in your own salvation, that it avails, that it is pertinent, to speak to you of God's part in it.*

This human Theory of getting rid of Sin by the joint operation of Christ's atonement, and man's "works of obedience," has not, and cannot have anything at all to do with eternal life *in* Christ. Nevertheless it is by means of this confusion, that so many keep on the broad way that leadeth unto destruction, whether they be reckless, or devout, Protestants or Catholics. Satan could not uproot and destroy the truth and promises of God in his Son, but his plan from beginning, was to fuse and make an alloy of one or more fundamental truths, and so confound them, that the result should be a fatal doctrine upheld by an ecclesiastical system of his own.

Having thus led his own seed to preach "another Gospel," it was Satan's next object to increase and to deepen deception by a further admixture of the old Covenant with the New.

The New Testament speaks and instructs us, res-

---

* "See Discourses to mixed Congregations." p. 132. By Dr. Newman, who chooses to believe that this is the Gospel the Redeemer commanded his Apostles to preach.

pecting a Ministry, consisting of local Rules, Elders, Bishops or Overseers; teachers, pastors, evangelists, and others; for the perfecting of the saints, for the work of the ministry, and for the general welfare, order, and edification " of the body of Christ," the Spirit, and not man, " dividing to every man," in every Church or Congregation, " severally as *he* will." In the xii of the first epistle to the Corinthians, and in other Scriptures, the reader may easily learn everything concerning " spiritual gifts," respecting which, the Apostle told *all* the Corinthian believers, that " he would not have them ignorant." St. Paul speaks of *all* the children of the kingdom, as " a holy priesthood," able to offer spiritual sacrifices acceptable unto God ; not through, or by means of an *especial* human order of priests but through Jesus Christ their High Priest *in heaven.* " Ye are," adds the same Apostle, "a chosen genera- tion, a royal priesthood, an holy nation, a peculiar people," in the midst of which, the promised Spirit ought to govern, gifting some, in an especial manner for ministering to every congregation that meets in the name of the Lord. It is clear that the New Testa- ment speaks of a ministry, ordered and variously gifted by the Spirit of God. Now the next thing the sower of the Tares did, was, as soon as possible, to displace the order and gifts of the Spirit, in the midst of the good seed, or children of the kingdom. This he accomplished by means of his own seed, which he sowed not elsewhere, but in the same field, and scat- tered among the Wheat.

A particular caste of individuals were soon raised up, who separated themselves from the general mass of Tares, and constituted themselves *Priests*, somewhat after the pattern of the Old Testament priesthood. This Caste has wrought wonderfully ever since, and as al-

ready observed, have been the chief instruments used
by him who raised them up for the confusion of the
first fundamental truths and promises of the present
Dispensation, and which they have accomplished by an
unrighteous amalgamation of the First and Second
Covenants, resulting in a third, which ignores both
the letter and spirit of God's Word, and which none
of the Apostles could now recognise as the everlasting
Gospel of Jesus Christ, which they had preached
and died for. St. Paul, who wrote very fully to the Hebrews respecting the distinctive character of the First
and Second Covenant of God, alludes to the Old Testament as "ready to vanish away," it having been a
pattern or a shadow, not of another *earthly* order
which was to belong to the New Covenant, but of the
"*heavenly* things" of the New Testament, in which
the children of the kingdom, are constituted the tem-
ple of the Holy Ghost, a spiritual house, built of living
stones, and founded on Christ, the chief corner-stone.
If the reader will carefully read the 8th, 9th, and
10th of Hebrews he will readily apprehend what is
here meant. Now in order to hide and confuse this
order of truth, so *plainly* revealed in God's Word, the
new and humanly devised priesthood, soon established
a totally new covenant which Satan owns and not God.
They first of all decreed and insisted that certain ma-
terial acts, or symbols, were not a mere outward sign
of what the believer already possessed as a child of God,
in Christ, but that the sign itself had, and did bestow
the grace it represented. This was a great triumph,
because it led men and sinners in need of redemption,
to rely on types and signs, instead of the substance.
This device is now so ancient, and so ingrafted by cus-
tom and tradition in the conviction of many, that it
deceives even those who are anxious, not to be de-

ceived. Thus, in the New Testament we find that none were baptized, save those who believed and declared themselves followers of Christ and of his Gospel. Neither did the Apostles, in any of their epistles, reprove parents for neglecting the baptism of their children at any age. We are not here either ignoring or advocating infant baptism, but if infants were "born again" when baptized, the truth would be of the very first importance, and the neglect thereof, tremendous, and the Scriptures would have given us the *plainest* precepts respecting this beautiful ordinance; yet all that God is pleased to tell us is, that "He that *believeth*, and is baptized shall be saved." The new order of priests however, soon disposed of the new birth in Christ, by declaring that infants are born again when baptized, and then and there become children of God; but in the day of judgment we shall find that this, and every other device that man has invented shall be proved a falsehood, by the gracious words pronounced by the Saviour himself in respect of *all* infants, for "of such is the kingdom of heaven." St. Paul, writing on this very subject to the ancient Romans, begins his instruction by quoting two verses from the Old Testament:—

"Blessed are they whose iniquities are forgiven, and whose sins are covered. Blessed is the man to whom the Lord will not impute sin." Taking these two verses for his premisis, the Apostle asks: "Cometh this blessedness upon the circumcision, or upon the *un*-circumcision also; for we say that *faith* was reckoned to Abraham for righteousness? *How* was it reckoned? when he was *in* circumcision, or in *un*circumcision? *Not* in circumcision, but in *un*circumcision; and he recieved the *sign* of circumcision, a seal of the *righteousness of the faith*, which he had, yet being uncircumcised." This, like every Scripture on this simple subject, is very plain. But it was the Deceiver's object that the Priests of the Tares, should, as much as possible, get the good seed or children of the kingdom, under their dominion, and his success has been such, that the mind and judgment of the true disciples of Christ have been so warped and prejudiced, that many cannot read the Word of God without understanding it on this, and on many other points, according to the customs and traditions established by, and for, the mere professing Churches. So much so indeed, that they often get angry and intolerant towards those who do keep to the word of God. This perversion of one of the most impressive and beautiful types, was the commencement of what the deceived call, their "Sacramental system," of which the Word of God says nothing, and which Dr. Newman first heard of from one of his human authorities.

A tribe who constituted themselves a separate caste consisting of Pope, Cardinals, Archbishops, Priests, &c. necessarily required "Consecrated buildings," altars, candles, incense, and a daily sacrifice. To provide the latter, and as if to show his powers of deception, the "enemy" led his priests to believe and to preach that the Son of God was verily and bodily present in a "Consecrated wafer," and in some Consecrated wine. This device is called the "Real Presence" and constitutes an object of daily and hourly adoration. But finding nothing in the Word of God, to support this degraded and degrading notion, the Romish Priests, as usual, established it on their own authority, and at a Council called the Council of Trent, they decreed as follows:—

" Since in this divine sacrifice, which is performed in the mass, there is contained and sacrificed without the shedding of his blood, that selfsame Christ, who offered himself up by the shedding of his blood on the altar *(sic)* of the Cross, the holy Council *(!)* teaches that this sacrifice is truly propitiatory."

Some opposition was feared, and some of the "good seed" did, in a feeble way, testify against this device, hence the following Canon was added:—

"If any one shall say that there is not in the New Testament a visible priesthood, or that there is no power in it of consecrating and offering the very body and blood of the Lord, and of remitting and retaining sins, but only an office and mere ministry of preaching the Gospel, or that those who do not preach the Gospel are not priests, let him be anathema."

The "children of the kingdom," as remarked above, made but a feeble resistance, for Satan had caused many divisions among them, one of his earliest devices having been, to divide and weaken. Moreover many had become worldly, and careless of discipline among themselves, while others, allured by the eloquence, zeal, the real or apparent sincerity of some of the Priests, soon joined this system, as is the case in our days, when so many exemplary children of God, abide in ecclesiastical establishments systematically allied with the World; which some would, nevertheless abandon; but the fear of man, the reproach of friends or relatives, and the love of family traditions, is stronger in some, than their love of unqualified discipleship. Moreover, through the grace of God, many of the Priests and their followers involved in the system, come to the knowledge of the truth as it is in Christ, and this is complacently accepted as sufficient proof that their place is the right one. In a natural point of view, the system

we have been endeavouring to describe, has so enlarged
and magnified itself, that this fact, together with its
buildings, splendid pictures, and beautiful music, are all
accepted by the ignorant, as things that must be most
appropriate to the Church of God, and unless the
Reformation, incomplete as it was, had brought some
people to refuse and to ignore the chief devices of this
human system, it is really difficult to imagine when,
where, or by whom, the Gospel of Christ would now
be preached; for at one period the whole world was
under the dominion of false christians, and their Priests
had attained to such influence and authority that they
were able, with perfect impunity to massacre, burn or
imprison, hundreds of thousands, who by the grace of
God manifested, even a moderate desire to be guided
by His written Word. Another point worthy of notice
is, that many, and chiefly those in "holy orders," are
sincere in their delusion, and blind to their deadly state.
The Deceiver could do very little with them, as his
.agents, unless some of them were deceived into a sincere belief in themselves and in their system. The following quotation from the conclusion of a sermon, will
show both the sincerity and sheer nonsense some
Priests believe and trust in. Alluding to the hour of
death he says:—

It will be a blessed thing, in your last hour, when flesh
and heart are failing, in midst of the pain, the weariness,
the restlessness, the prostration of strength, the ex-
haustion of spirits, which then will be your portion,
it will be blessed indeed to have her (Mary) at your
side, more tender than a mother, to nurse you, and to
whisper peace. It will be most blessed, when the evil
one is making his last effort, when he is coming on
you in his might to pluck you away from your Father's
hand, if he can; it will be blessed indeed if Jesus,

Joseph, and Mary are there waiting to shield you from his assaults and to receive your soul. If they are there, all is there; Angels are there, Saints are there, heaven is there, heaven is begun in you, and the devil has no part in you. That dread day may be sooner or later, you may be taken away young, you may live to fourscore, you may die in your bed, you may die in .the open field, but if Mary intercedes for you, that day will find you watching and ready. All things will be fixed to secure your salvation; all dangers will be foreseen, all obstacles removed, all aids provided. The hour will come, and in a moment you will be translated beyond fear and risk, you will be translated into a new state where sin is not, nor ignorance of the future, but perfect faith, serene joy, and assurance and love everlasting.

Jesu, Joseph, and Mary, I offer you my soul and my heart!

Jesu, Joseph, and Mary, assist me in my last agony!

Jesu, Joseph, and Mary, let me breathe out my soul with you in peace! *

" Go and cry unto the gods which ye have chosen; let them deliver you in the time of your tribulation."

Jud. x. 14.

It is no marvel if some are profoundly deceived; for Satan himself, transformed into an angel of light, hath transformed many "false apostles and deceitful workers into, *Apostles of Christ.*" "Therefore." adds St. Paul, "it is no great thing if his ministers also, be transformed as the ministers *of righteousness.*"

We cannot, in conclusion, forebear once to repeat, that the influence of this spurious Christianity, sown

---

* Discourses addressed to Mixed Congregations. By Dr. Newman.

and developed by "the enemy," has been most disas-
trous to the children of the kingdom : It has destroyed
their united testimony respecting sin, righteousness
and judgment. Nevertheless the Lord knoweth them
that are his, and none of them shall be lost. The good
seed is still sown, and many believe unto righteousness.
But who can now conceive or imagine the diversity,
the power, the subtilty of the falsehoods that shall be
revealed, in the day when God shall judge the secrets
of men by Jesus Christ!

THE END.

www.ingramcontent.com/pod-product-compliance
Lightning Source LLC
Chambersburg PA
CBHW031749090426
42739CB00008B/947